What Is a Wheel and Axle?

By Lloyd G. Douglas

Welcome Books

Children's Press®
A Division of Scholastic Inc.
New York / Toronto / London / Auckland / Sydney
Mexico City / New Delhi / Hong Kong
Danbury, Connecticut

Photo Credits: Cover © Paul Almasy/Corbis; pp. 5, 7, 9, 11, 13, 15, 17, 19, 21 by Maura B. McConnell
Contributing Editor: Jennifer Silate
Book Design: Mindy Liu

Library of Congress Cataloging-in-Publication Data

Douglas, Lloyd G.
What is a wheel and axle? / by Lloyd G. Douglas.
    p. cm. -- (Simple machines)
Summary: Introduces the wheel and axle as a simple machine that can make it easier to move heavy objects, as well as to flatten dough.
ISBN 0-516-23962-7 -- ISBN 0-516-24027-7
1. Wheels--Juvenile literature. 2. Axles--Juvenile literature. [1. Wheels. 2. Axles.] I. Title.

TJ181.5 .D68 2002
621.8'11--dc21

2002001412

Contents

This is a wheel and **axle**.

The axle is a rod.

It goes through a wheel.

The wheel can turn.

Wheels and axles are used in many different ways.

A **wheelbarrow** has a wheel and axle.

A wheelbarrow can hold many things.

The wheel and axle makes moving things easier.

A **rolling pin** is a wheel and axle.

The handles of the rolling pins are the axle.

The pin works like a wheel.

A rolling pin is used to flatten **dough**.

The pin is rolled back and forth on its axle.

There are wheels and axles all around us.

This wagon has two axles and four wheels.

RADIO FLYER

Wheels and axles are very helpful **simple machines**.

21

New Words

axle (**ak**-suhl) a rod in the center of a wheel, around which the wheel turns

dough (**doh**) a soft, sticky mixture of flour, water, and other things, used to make bread, cookies, muffins, and other food

rolling pin (**rohl**-ing **pin**) a cylinder, often made of wood, that is used to flatten out dough

simple machines (**sim**-puhl muh-**sheenz**) basic mechanical devices that make work easier

wheelbarrow (**weel**-ba-roh) a small cart with one wheel at the front, often used to carry things around in yards or gardens

To Find Out More

Books

Machines We Use
by Sally Hewitt
Grolier Publishing

Simple Machines
by Deborah Hodge
Kids Can Press

Web Site

Dirtmeister: Simple Machines
http://teacher.scholastic.com/dirtrep/simple/index.htm
Learn about simple machines on this fun Web site.

Index

About the Author
Lloyd G. Douglas is an editor and writer of children's books.

Reading Consultants
Kris Flynn, Coordinator, Small School District Literacy, The San Diego County Office of Education

Shelly Forys, Certified Reading Recovery Specialist, W.J. Zahnow Elementary School, Waterloo, IL

Sue McAdams, Former President of the North Texas Reading Council of the IRA, and Early Literacy Consultant, Dallas, TX